IN COLONIAL NEW ENGLAND

IN COLONIAL NEW ENGLAND

by Deborah Kent

BENCHMARK BOOKS

MARSHALL CAVENDISH
NEW YORK

ACKNOWLEDGMENT

*For his generous assistance and expert advice, the author wishes to thank
Clarence G. Seckel, Jr., Curriculum Coordinator in the Social Studies,
East Saint Louis School District 189, East Saint Louis, Illinois.*

Benchmark Books
Marshall Cavendish Corporation
99 White Plains Road
Tarrytown, New York 10591-9001

• • •

Library of Congress Cataloging-in-Publication Data
Kent, Deborah
In Colonial New England / Deborah Kent
p. cm—(How we lived)
Includes bibliographical references and index.
Summary: Describes various aspects of the life of early settlers in New England
including their homes, schools, religion, work and community.
ISBN 0-7614-0905-X (lib.bdg.)
1. New England—Social life and customs—To 1775—Juvenile literature.   2. Frontier and pioneer life—
New England—Juvenile literature.   [1. New England—Social life and customs—to 1775.
2. Frontier and pioneer life—New England.   3. Pioneers.]   I. Title.   II. Series.
F7.K46   2000   98-7780   974′.02—dc21   CIP   AC

• • •

Printed in Hong Kong
1 3 5 6 4 2

• • •

Book Designer: Judith Turziano
Photo Researcher: Debbie Needleman

• • •

PHOTO CREDITS
Front cover: Courtesy of John Lewis Stage/The Image Bank; pages 2–3, 32–33, 34, 42–43, 57: Stock Montage;
pages 6–7, 9, 11, 27, 29, 35, 39, 45, 52–53: North Wind Picture Archives; page 8: The Detroit Institute of Art, Founders
Society Purchase, Gibbs-Williams Fund; pages 12–13: Culver Pictures; page 14: Derek Redfearn/The Image Bank;
pages 15, 16: Steve Dunwell/The Image Bank; page 20: Jacqui Hurst/Corbis; page 21: Worcester Art Museum,
Worcester, MA, Sarah C. Garver Fund; page 22: The Connecticut Historical Society, Hartford,CT;
pages 24–25: Fine Arts Museum of San Francisco, Gift of Mr. & Mrs. John D. Rockefeller 3rd, 1979.7.3 (Detail);
page 40: Nancy Carter/North Wind Picture Archives; page 46: Cigna Museum and Art Collection;
page 49: Private Collection/Bridgeman Art Library, London/New York; page 55: Massachusetts Historical
Society; page 58: Gift of Joseph W., William B., and Edward H. R. Revere, Courtesy Museum of
Fine Arts, Boston, Acc#30.781; page 59: R.H. Love Galleries, Chicago

Contents

1

A Stern and Rock-Bound Coast

*"In two or three months' time half of [our] company
died, especially in January and February, being the depth
of winter, and wanting houses and other comforts;…
So as there died sometimes two or three of a day…that of one
hundred and odd persons, scarce fifty remained. And of these,
in the time of most distress, there were but six or seven sound
persons who…fetched them wood, made them fires, dressed
them meat, made their beds, washed their loathsome clothes,
clothed and unclothed them. In a word, did all the homely
and necessary offices for them which dainty and queasy
stomachs cannot endure to bear named; and all this willingly
and cheerfully, without any grudging in the least, showing
herein their true love unto their friends and brethren."*

—WILLIAM BRADFORD, GOVERNOR
OF PLYMOUTH PLANTATION

With these words William Bradford recalled the grim winter of 1620–1621 at Plymouth Plantation. Plymouth was the first English settlement in the present-day state of Massachusetts. Today most Americans know its original settlers as the Pilgrims, the people who celebrated the first Thanksgiving. William Bradford, governor of Plymouth Plantation, kept a detailed record of the colony's early history. His account gives us a glimpse into the everyday lives of the colony's men, women, and children.

In 1630, ten years after Plymouth Plantation was founded, several more shiploads of colonists reached Massachusetts. Wave after wave of newcomers followed. Many were Puritans, members of a religious group who sought the freedom to worship God as they chose. Others were poor people who wanted to improve their lives. They hoped to become successful farmers or fishermen. A few were brought against their will, as slaves. During their first years in the New World, most of the colonists found little but hunger and cold. Many died.

This portrait of a slave was painted in the late 1700s by famous colonial artist John Singleton Copley. Slavery was made legal in the Massachusetts Bay Colony in 1641.

As time passed, however, the colonists gained a firm footing in their adopted land. Settlements sprang up throughout the region known as New England. Today New England includes the states of Massachusetts, Rhode Island, Connecticut, Vermont, New Hampshire, and Maine.

At first the colonists clustered along the New England coast. Gradually they pushed deeper and deeper inland.

The Pilgrims first lived in dugouts, holes cut in the hillsides and covered with strips of bark. But they couldn't live in these "smoaky homes" for long. They needed permanent shelters, safe from the harsh weather and the "wolves who sat upon their tayles and grinned at us."

They cleared forests to make way for farms, villages, and towns.

More than a century after the first New Englanders arrived, a British poet named Felicia Hemans wrote about their heroic struggles. She described the landing of the Pilgrims on "a stern and rock-bound coast." The coast of New England was indeed rugged. The winters were fiercely cold, and the stony soil fought the farmer's plow. But New England also offered splendid gifts. The coastal waters teemed with cod and other fish. Deer, moose, and game birds flourished in the woods. The massive trunks

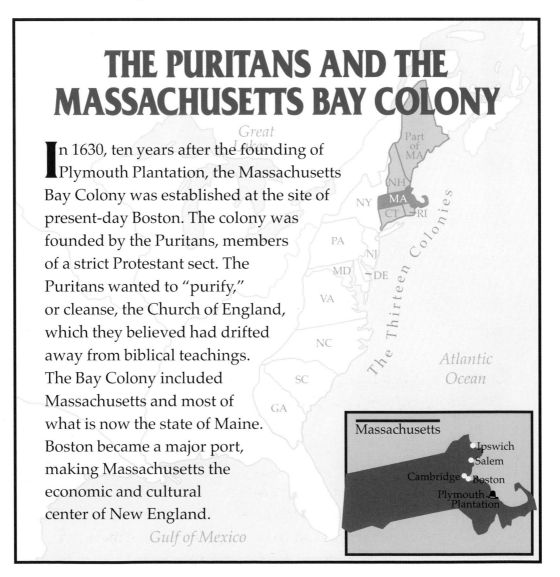

THE PURITANS AND THE MASSACHUSETTS BAY COLONY

In 1630, ten years after the founding of Plymouth Plantation, the Massachusetts Bay Colony was established at the site of present-day Boston. The colony was founded by the Puritans, members of a strict Protestant sect. The Puritans wanted to "purify," or cleanse, the Church of England, which they believed had drifted away from biblical teachings. The Bay Colony included Massachusetts and most of what is now the state of Maine. Boston became a major port, making Massachusetts the economic and cultural center of New England.

The Pilgrims had no idea what they would face in the New World.
But their hard work and determination pulled them through.

of ancient trees provided timber for carpenters and shipbuilders.

The colonists brought many customs and beliefs with them when they crossed the Atlantic. But New England made them adapt to a life they had never known before. With new skills and resources they built houses, made clothing, and raised food. Along the stern and rock-bound coast they created a home for themselves and for future generations.

2
Home and Hearth

*"The chimney is large, with an oven at each end of him;
he is so large that we can place our kettle within the [fireplace].
We can brew and bake and boil our kettle all at once in him."*

—A LETTER FROM JOHN WYNTER OF MAINE
TO HIS BROTHER IN ENGLAND, 1634

WIGWAMS AND SALTBOXES

When the first colonists reached New England they did not find an uninhabited land. Native American people from several small tribal groups hunted in the forests and gathered clams along the shores. The colonists thought of their neighbors, the Wampanoags, Narragansetts, and other Indians, as lost "heathen" souls in need of salvation. However the Indians had many skills that the colonists needed in order to survive.

The Indians moved often and rarely built permanent homes. They made their shelters quickly of branches plastered with mud. The colonists called these Indian dwellings wigwams. During their first winter at Plymouth, the colonists constructed their homes in much the same way.

The first colonists lived in wigwams like this one at Plymouth Plantation. It was a design borrowed from the Indians.

They wove branches into a rough circular frame and daubed it with mud to fill in the cracks. These "English wigwams," as they were nicknamed, were miserably cold in the icy winter. They were tiny, crowded, and smoky from the cooking fire.

As soon as they could, the colonists set to work on more permanent homes. At first they built small houses of wood. Later they also used brick and stone. Gradually New England homes grew larger and more substantial.

The most important room in a New England house was the "common room," and the most important feature of the common

You could stand inside the fireplace in the common room. The lugpole had many hooks so several dishes could cook at the same time, and there often was a small oven for a baking.

room was the fireplace. Through the long winter months the fireplace was the family's only source of heat. Parents and children spent as much time as they could in its circle of warmth.

The size of the fireplace reflected its central role in family life. In some homes it measured ten feet across. Children liked to sit on the hearth in the evening, watching the dancing flames. On a clear night they gazed up the chimney at the glittering stars in the sky.

In the earliest houses the common room served as kitchen, living room, and even bedroom. A "pull-up bed" was attached to the wall with hinges.

A hutch, or cupboard, displays the family's prized pewter and pottery.

During the day the bed was folded up and out of the way. At night it was extended into the room so the master and mistress of the house could sleep in comfort near the fire. The children usually slept upstairs in the loft, a tiny room under the roof.

Glass windows were unknown in the early days of the New England colonies. Windows were made of paper soaked in cooking grease. The grease made the paper translucent, so that light shone through it. These paper windows were not much good at keeping out the cold. Eventually glassmakers set up workshops in the colonies. By the middle of the eighteenth century most people who lived in towns and cities had glass windows. The windows did not slide up and down as they do today. Instead they opened on hinges, swinging inward like double doors.

By the late 1600s the typical New England house was a square, two-story structure with a steeply sloping roof. The house somewhat resembled a type of box in which salt once was sold. For this reason these New England dwellings are often called saltbox houses.

THE GROANING BOARD

The common room of a New England house served so many purposes that it was always crowded. The colonists found clever ways to make the best use of their limited space. Instead of a dining table, which would be in the way when the meal was finished, the family set up a board-table at mealtimes. The board-table was a long, narrow plank. It rested on trestles, or supports, somewhat like modern sawhorses. The family sat along the board on backless benches called forms. When they were not needed, the board-table and forms were stacked against a wall.

During the 1600s most colonists ate from carved wooden bowls known as trenchers. Trenchers were either round or square. Usually two people sitting side by side shared a trencher between them. Ale or springwater was served in a large wooden mug. Everyone drank from the same one, passing it up and down the table. Doubtless they passed an array of germs back and forth along with it.

In 1633 John Winthrop, governor of the Massachusetts Bay Colony, received a surprise from England. Packed in a fine leather case was a lone metal fork. The governor's fork was the first such utensil ever seen in the English colonies. The early colonists used only knives and spoons. Forks did not become popular until the 1700s. In their absence, people ate with their spoons or knives, or with their fingers. Every household kept a generous supply of linen napkins.

By the mid-1700s most wooden trenchers were replaced by bowls and plates made of pewter. Pewter is a metal made by blending a small amount of copper and antimony with tin. Plates, bowls, pitchers, mugs, and spoons made of pewter were very popular in New England. They were simply designed and could have either a dull or highly polished finish. Homemakers proudly displayed their pewter on a chest of drawers in the common room.

Families in large towns such as Boston, Massachusetts, and Newport, Rhode Island, could buy some of their food in shops. Butchers sold meat and bakers sold fresh bread. Some shops carried imported foods, luxuries such as ginger, oranges, limes, tea, and chocolate.

But most of the colonists did not buy their food from stores. Nine of every ten New Englanders lived on a farm or in a tiny village. These country people raised most of their food themselves. Their cows provided milk, which the women and older girls made into cheese and butter. The

A GIFT FROM THE INDIANS

The early colonists found the Indians tilling fields of maize, or corn. Corn soon became one of the colonists' staple foods. They ate it roasted and dried. They ground the kernels into meal for bread. A special treat was a cornmeal dessert:

INDIAN PUDDING

3 cups milk

1/3 cup molasses

1/3 cup yellow cornmeal

1 beaten egg

1/4 cup sugar

2 teaspoons butter

1/2 teaspoon ground ginger

1/2 teaspoon ground cinnamon

1/4 teaspoon salt

In a deep skillet combine the milk and molasses. Using a wooden spoon, blend in the cornmeal. Cook this mixture at moderate heat for about ten minutes. Stir frequently. It will gradually become thick and hard to stir. Turn off the heat and let the mixture cool slightly. In a mixing bowl, combine the egg, sugar, butter, spices, and salt. Add the hot cornmeal mixture a few spoonfuls at a time. Stir until smooth. Pour into a 2-quart casserole and bake uncovered at 300 degrees Fahrenheit for about 1 1/2 hours. Indian pudding is great served hot with ice cream or whipped cream!

children collected eggs from the henhouse every morning. The slaughtering of a pig was a special occasion. A fully grown hog provided pork, ham, bacon, and sausage—enough meat to last all winter. The colonists supplemented their diet by hunting, fishing, and gathering wild nuts and fruits.

Food preparation was a tremendous amount of work, most of which fell to the woman of the house. During the 1760s Mary Holyoke, the wife of a doctor in Salem, Massachusetts, kept a record of her household chores and projects. In the course of one year she "sowed sweet marjoram.… Sowed peas.…Sowed cauliflower.…Pulled first radishes. Set out turnips.… Cut 36 asparagus.…Bought 11 ducks.…Bought a doe rabbit [which] brought forth 6 young ones, 3 of which died.…Killed the pig, weighed 164 pounds.… Salted pork.…Preserved quinces. Made syrup of cores and parings."

As John Wynter wrote in his letter to his brother, colonial cooks prepared nearly the whole meal in the fireplace. Pots and kettles hung above the flames from a heavy bar called a lug pole. Many pots had short legs and could be set on top of the glowing coals. More hot coals were heaped upon the lid. Biscuits, bread, and even pies were baked in these "ovens."

Meat and vegetables were usually cooked together in a large hanging pot. The mixture was served as a stew to be eaten with a spoon. A large piece of meat could be skewered on an iron prong called a spit. By cranking a handle the cook turned the spit and roasted the meat evenly.

FROM HOMESPUN TO HIGH FASHION

One piece of furniture found in most New England common rooms was a spinning wheel. The spinning wheel, a machine for making thread, was operated by hand. Colonial families earned extra money by selling this thread to local weavers. The weavers in turn made it into cloth. Sometimes this homespun thread was made from wool. More often it was made from the fibers of a plant called flax.

Flax, a tall, graceful plant, was raised by many of the colonists. Carefully dried, crushed, and cleaned, the stalks of the flax plant could be split into thin fibers. These fibers were spun into linen thread. Women and girls spent many long hours at the spinning wheel every day. A foot pedal turned a large wooden wheel. This moving wheel pushed gears, which twirled a slender wooden spindle. The spindle's action twisted raw flax fibers into thread. To most New Englanders the thump of the pedal and the steady whir of the wheel were the comforting sounds of home.

Homespun thread varied greatly in quality. The coarsest flax thread

Much like combing hair, flax was "hackled" through the "hetchels,"
or pulled through a bed of nails to remove the husks and seeds.
Then it could be spun into linen thread.

was woven into a rough fabric known as tow. Tow clothing was chiefly
worn by slaves, hired servants, and the poorest farm families in the backcountry. A brand-new tow shirt was full of prickly spines from the flax
stems. Only repeated washings made the cloth softer and less scratchy.

Deerskin breeches and jackets were worn by both country folk and
towns-people. Deerskin is a soft, lightweight leather. To Europeans, clothes
made of deerskin symbolized life in the American wilderness.

The Puritans who founded Massachusetts disapproved of fancy clothes
or "immoderate dress." In 1634 Massachusetts passed a law forbidding
the purchase of garments trimmed with lace. Over the years that followed,
people were fined for wearing double ruffles, beaver hats, and gold and
silver buckles. Gradually people took these laws less seriously. In 1676
sixteen-year-old Hannah Lyman was charged with "wearing silk in a
flaunting way." She brazenly wore her offending silk outfit right into
the courtroom.

Not all colonists dressed in the plain style of the Puritans.
This portrait of John Freake, a Boston merchant, shows he preferred the
high style of the day: a lace collar, large cuffs, and silver buttons trimming
the coat. Freake also shows his wealth by wearing a large gold ring.
The Puritans would have disapproved.

*Two perfect little gentlemen, from their buckled shoes
to the wigs on their heads.*

By the late 1600s New Englanders were following the fashions set in faraway London. Women who could afford to do so wore rustling gowns of silk or satin. Colonial gentlemen adopted the English custom of wearing wigs. The fashion in wigs shifted from year to year. Sometimes they were made of horsehair or cow's tails. Sometimes the fashion called for human hair or dyed linen thread. But whatever the year, the wig was dusted with white powder. Wigs were expensive and messy. On hot days they made their wearers miserable beyond description. Yet they remained in style for nearly a century.

Like their fathers and uncles, boys as young as seven or eight had to wear wigs. In dress, as in nearly everything else, New England children were expected to be miniature replicas of the adults around them.

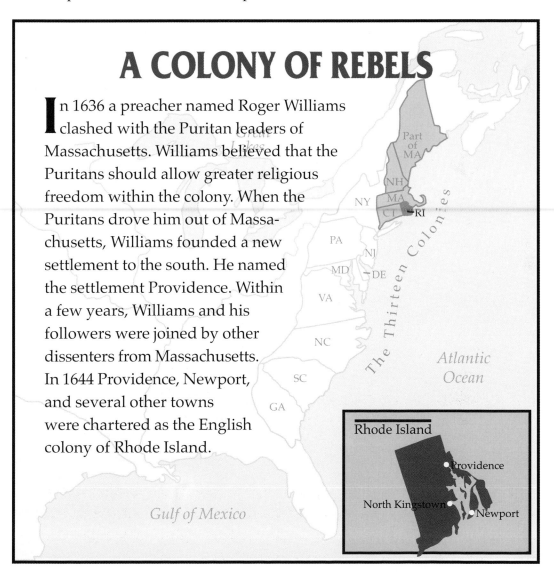

A COLONY OF REBELS

In 1636 a preacher named Roger Williams clashed with the Puritan leaders of Massachusetts. Williams believed that the Puritans should allow greater religious freedom within the colony. When the Puritans drove him out of Massachusetts, Williams founded a new settlement to the south. He named the settlement Providence. Within a few years, Williams and his followers were joined by other dissenters from Massachusetts. In 1644 Providence, Newport, and several other towns were chartered as the English colony of Rhode Island.

3

Seen and Not Heard

*"Surely there is in all children (though not alike)
a stubbornness and stoutness of mind arising from
natural pride which must in the first place be broken and
beaten down that so the foundation of their education
being laid in humility and tractableness other virtues
may in their time be built thereon."*

—THE REVEREND JOHN ROBINSON,
A MINISTER AT PLYMOUTH

BEATEN, BROKEN, AND BELOVED

Today parents and teachers try to help children express themselves. In colonial New England, however, children were raised very differently. When grown-ups were present a child was not to speak unless spoken to. Adults believed that children should be humble and submissive. They should put aside their earthly yearnings and prepare for the world to come.

The church was the center of life in early New England. Children were taught the Bible from the time they were three or four years old. Much of this religious teaching focused on the idea that human beings are sinful by nature. Temptation lurked everywhere. Children needed to fight their evil tendencies and strive all the time to improve themselves.

Like mothers and fathers everywhere, New England parents loved their children deeply. But their child-raising methods often seem cruel by today's standards. Whipping was considered a proper and necessary form of punishment. One Massachusetts woman described whipping a teenage servant named Dearlove, and added, "She hath never been whipped before, she says, since she was a child (what can her mother… have been about I wonder?)"

Despite their strict upbringing, New England children still managed to get into mischief. They threw stones, skipped school, and quarreled with their brothers and sisters. A Boston woman wrote about her grandson, who lived with her while he attended school, "Richard wears out nigh 12 pair of shoes a year. He brought 12 hankers [handkerchiefs] with him and they have all been lost long ago; and I have bought him 3 or 4 more at a time. His way is to tie knots at one end & beat the boys with them and then to lose them and he cares not a bit what I will say to him."

THE HORNBOOK AND THE QUILL

Since the Bible was so important in New England, children were expected to read it faithfully. Literacy—the ability to read and write—was considered essential. By the mid-1700s all of the New England colonies except

Rhode Island had laws calling for free public education. Every town of twenty families or more was required to open a school. In addition, New England had a number of private day schools and boarding schools.

Schools in the colonies were bleak and ill-equipped compared with those of today. There were no blackboards. Maps and charts were almost unknown. Even textbooks were few. Small children usually learned their letters from a "hornbook." A hornbook was not really a book. It was a single printed page backed by a sturdy board. A thin sheet of horn, the transparent outer layer of a cow's horn, protected the paper as a piece of plastic might today. The board, paper, and horn were fastened together by strips of brass at the edges. At the top of the hornbook was printed the alphabet. Below usually appeared simple syllables, such as "ab," "eb," and "ob." The Lord's Prayer or a verse from the Bible appeared at the bottom.

After a child mastered the hornbook it was time to move on to *The New England Primer*. This basic textbook was used throughout New England for more than a hundred years. It, too, began with the alphabet. Most letters were illustrated with a biblical reference. The primer started with

The Puritans thought that learning was very important.
They believed the Devil tricked people by keeping them in ignorance.
Education was a tool to fight the temptations of evil.

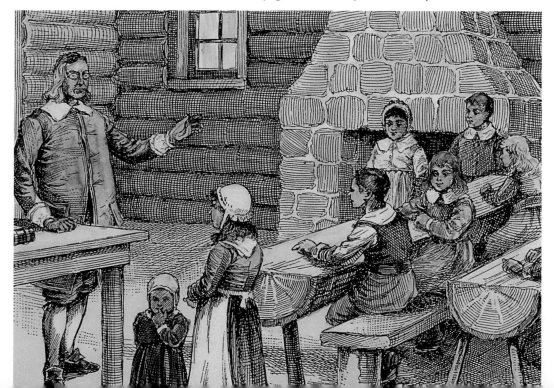

A: "In Adam's fall / We sinned all." There followed pages of Bible verses, prayers, and advice on leading a virtuous life. The familiar children's prayer that begins, "Now I lay me down to sleep…" appeared in *The New England Primer* more than two hundred years ago.

A few women ran schools for girls known as dame schools. But for the most part teaching was a man's profession. The schoolmaster's pay was low. Often he received eggs, cheese, bushels of corn, or other farm produce instead of money. During the winter the pupils' families cut and hauled firewood to heat the schoolhouse. In 1736 a court in West Hartford, Connecticut, ordered that any child whose parents failed to provide their share of logs be "barred from the fire."

When the schoolmaster entered the room all of the pupils had to rise respectfully. The master's authority was never to be questioned. He disciplined his pupils freely, in whatever way he saw fit. Whippings with a hickory or willow branch were a daily occurrence in many schoolrooms. But humiliation was a worse punishment than the sting of the switch. Children were sometimes forced to wear placards announcing their crimes. A boy who did not complete his math problems wore the label "idler." A girl who talked to the child behind her was "Pert-Miss-Prat-a-Pace."

Colonial children usually left school once they learned to read, write, and do basic arithmetic. At that point many children left home to become apprentices. An apprentice was under a legal contract to serve his or her master for a certain number of years. The apprenticeship usually lasted at least four or five years, but sometimes continued until the boy or girl reached twenty-one. The master was responsible for teaching the apprentice a skilled trade. Boys might learn to be blacksmiths, printers, shoemakers, or joiners (cabinetmakers). Girls learned such trades as weaving and dressmaking.

A few young men in the colonies had the opportunity to pursue higher education. An educated man was one with a thorough knowledge of Latin, and perhaps ancient Greek as well. (The study of these languages was thought improper for girls.) Boys who studied Latin were obliged to learn long passages by heart, often without the slightest idea what the strange words meant.

Graceful handwriting was another proof that a person had a good education. Penmanship was an art to be mastered. "Try to mend your hand in writing every day using all the opportunities you can possibly get," a Massachusetts farmer urged his son, who was away at Princeton College in New Jersey. "Observe strictly the gentlemen's method of writing, it may be of service to you: you can scarce conceive what a vast disadvantage it will be to leave the College and not be able to write and spell well. Learn to write a pretty fine hand as you may have occasion."

The pens used by the colonists were goose feathers or quills, carefully pared to a sharp point. The point was then dipped into liquid ink. Children had to bring their own ink to school. Generally they made it at home by mixing water with a store-bought powder. In Vermont and Maine settlers learned to make ink by boiling the bark of the swamp maple.

Schooling was important to

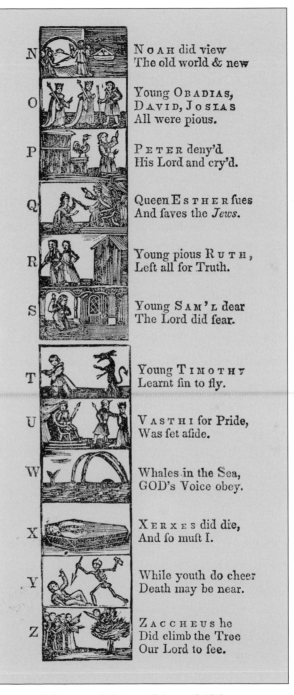

Along with teaching children how to read, primers gave lessons in religion and good behavior.

the New Englanders. But even more important was the daily round of chores. Children played an essential part in the world of work.

FROM SUNUP TILL DARK

Most New England children were busy with chores all day long. Each child provided an extra pair of hands that could be put to good use. Even children of four or five had work to do in a New England household.

One of the chores reserved for the smallest children was weeding the flax plants. Newly sprouted flax plants are very delicate and must not be stepped on. Agile children with tiny feet were the least likely to cause harm. Children walked barefoot among the rows of plants, pulling weeds so the flax could grow.

Children were also a help when it came time to spin the flax fibers into thread. Some girls of six could already operate a spinning wheel, though they had to stand on a footstool to reach it. Girls sewed, kneaded bread, and tended their younger brothers and sisters. But spinning was considered the finest of feminine accomplishments.

Girls performed most of their chores indoors. Boys, on the other hand, chiefly helped with the outdoor work of caring for crops and livestock. David and John Brainerd, who later became missionaries to the Indians, wrote of growing up in colonial Connecticut:

"[The boy] must rise early and make himself useful before he went to school, must be diligent there in study, and [be] promptly home to do chores at evening. His whole time out of school must be filled up with some service, such as bringing in fuel for the day, cutting potatoes for the sheep, feeding the swine, watering the horses, picking the berries, gathering the vegetables, spooling the yarn [for spinning]. He was expected never to be reluctant and not often tired."

Even when the weather drove him indoors, the boy had work to do. He pulled out his jackknife and whittled a chunk of wood. Boys made wooden spoons, bowls, and breadboards. Their whittling produced combs for cleaning wool and an assortment of parts for the spinning wheel. Metal

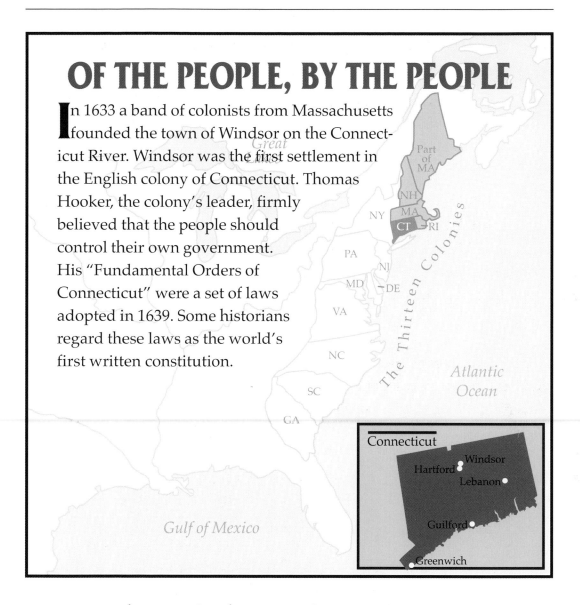

OF THE PEOPLE, BY THE PEOPLE

In 1633 a band of colonists from Massachusetts founded the town of Windsor on the Connecticut River. Windsor was the first settlement in the English colony of Connecticut. Thomas Hooker, the colony's leader, firmly believed that the people should control their own government. His "Fundamental Orders of Connecticut" were a set of laws adopted in 1639. Some historians regard these laws as the world's first written constitution.

was so scarce that even door hinges and fastenings for cupboards were whittled from wood. Boys usually kept the habit of whittling for a lifetime. Visitors to New England noted that the men always carried their jack-knives with them. They would work on a spoon or a spade handle in any quiet moment.

David and John Brainerd wrote that "the [colonial] boy was taught that laziness was the worst form of original sin." This attitude toward work sprang from the strict Puritan religion, which was the bedrock of early New England.

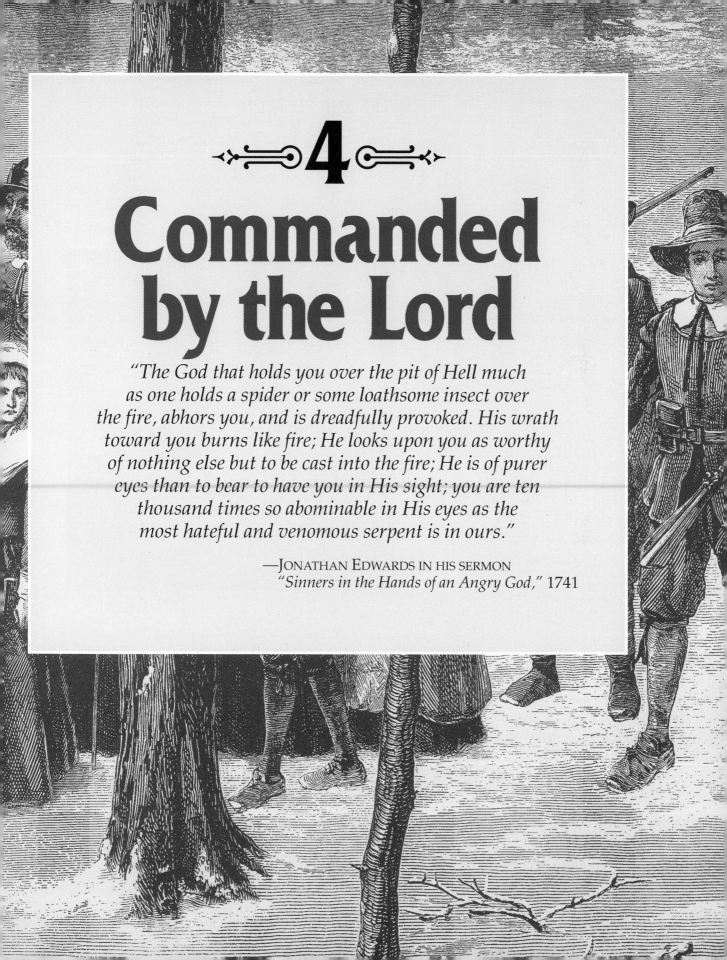

4
Commanded by the Lord

"The God that holds you over the pit of Hell much as one holds a spider or some loathsome insect over the fire, abhors you, and is dreadfully provoked. His wrath toward you burns like fire; He looks upon you as worthy of nothing else but to be cast into the fire; He is of purer eyes than to bear to have you in His sight; you are ten thousand times so abominable in His eyes as the most hateful and venomous serpent is in ours."

—JONATHAN EDWARDS IN HIS SERMON
"Sinners in the Hands of an Angry God," 1741

SINNERS AND SERMONS

The Puritans came to Massachusetts with one clear purpose. They wanted to build a godly society, one that would set an example for all people to follow. They hoped that by living strictly according to the Bible's teachings they would create the Kingdom of God on earth.

For the Puritans, religious life was far more than church attendance on Sundays. The Bible directed everything they did, from planting their corn to raising their children. They lived in fear of God's wrath and in the hope of salvation through His mercy.

"Though I am thus well in body yet I question whether my soul doth prosper as my body doth," wrote Samuel Mather of Massachusetts. "I perceive yet to this very day, little growth in grace; and this makes me question whether grace be in my heart or no." Samuel was the son of the famous Puritan preacher and writer Cotton Mather. When he wrote these troubled words to his father, Samuel was only twelve years old.

Cotton Mather believed his life was "a continual conversation with heaven." At first he didn't want to be a minister because of a speech impediment. A friend convinced him to change his mind. Mather became one of the most respected preachers of his time.

Samuel Mather's letter reflects the way the Puritans searched their souls, striving to find favor in the Lord's eyes. All around them lay the Devil's snares, threatening to lure them away from God's path. Dancing, games, and fancy clothes were all sinful. Devout Puritans worried each time such things led them astray.

The Lord's will was explained to the people of New England by their Puritan ministers. It was the minister's duty to insure that everyone learned and followed the Scriptures. At church on Sundays he (all Puritan ministers were men) tried to set a tone that would carry his flock safely past temptation. Yet despite the best efforts of their preachers, the early New Englanders had the usual range of human failings. Some stole, some drank, some were lazy and refused to work. There were even those who did not go to church at all.

By today's standards, Puritan church services, or "meetings," were a dreary business indeed. We can well understand why some New Englanders chose to stay at home. But to most of the colonists, going to church was a special occasion. It was a welcome break in a week filled with endless hard work. Even more important, it was a time when they renewed their connection with the Almighty.

The thump of the drum called worshippers from miles around. In some towns it was illegal to skip the Sunday service. Those caught sleeping in were given a heavy fine.

A DAY OF REST

Some New England churches summoned the congregation by the ringing of a bell. Some announced services by beating a drum. At a few churches a deacon blew on a large conch shell. The blast must have sounded like the trumpet that the Puritans expected to hear on the Day of Judgment.

As they filed into the church, the colonists took their assigned places. Deacons, or church officials, sat in the front rows below the pulpit. On one side of the central aisle sat the men, and across from them sat the women and girls. Indians and African Americans of both sexes climbed to the gallery beneath the rafters. Anyone who sat in the wrong section could be fined.

Though Puritan girls sat with their mothers, boys had a section all to themselves. In some churches they sat in the back. In others they were seated on the stairs to the gallery. Wherever they were, the boys were sometimes restless and disruptive. Any misbehavior during the service was a serious offense. A boy could be taken before the town magistrate and his parents forced to pay a fine. One Connecticut boy was charged with "smiling and laughing and enticing of others to the same evil.… Pulling the hair of his neighbor Benoni Simkins in the time of public worship. Throwing Sister Penticost Perkins on the ice, it being Sabbath day, between the meeting house and his place of abode." Surely the deacons were shocked. But the antics of the accused were probably a welcome diversion for the other boys during the service.

Service in a Puritan church lasted from nine o'clock in the morning until midafternoon. The sermon could stretch on for three or four hours. The minister sometimes spent an hour offering up a single prayer. Hymnals were scarce. A deacon called out the words to each hymn, line by line, and the congregation sang as he prompted. There was no church organ to help the singers stay on pitch. The result, according to a clergyman in the 1720s, was "a horrid medley of confused and disorderly noises." Some worshippers even suggested that this "music" was an insult to the Almighty.

REACHING NORTHWARD

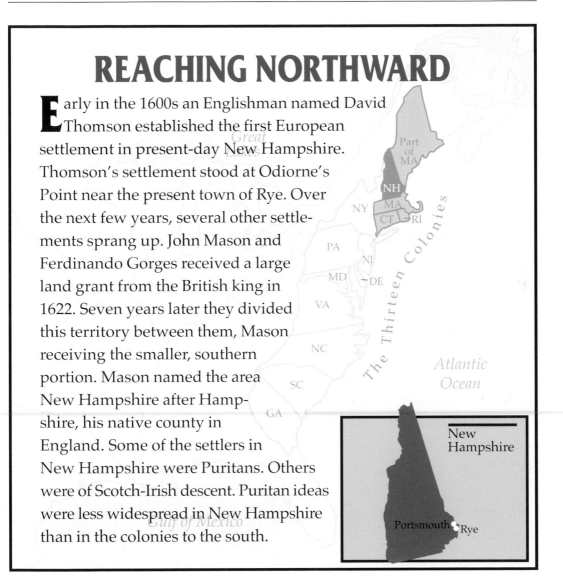

Early in the 1600s an Englishman named David Thomson established the first European settlement in present-day New Hampshire. Thomson's settlement stood at Odiorne's Point near the present town of Rye. Over the next few years, several other settlements sprang up. John Mason and Ferdinando Gorges received a large land grant from the British king in 1622. Seven years later they divided this territory between them, Mason receiving the smaller, southern portion. Mason named the area New Hampshire after Hampshire, his native county in England. Some of the settlers in New Hampshire were Puritans. Others were of Scotch-Irish descent. Puritan ideas were less widespread in New Hampshire than in the colonies to the south.

New England churches were unheated. During the winter months the congregation shivered in the bitter cold. Some people brought "warming stoves," metal boxes filled with hot coals, which they placed between their feet. Some came to church with their dogs, which lay on their feet to keep them warm. Every so often a dogfight broke out, and the troublemakers were chased outside.

At noon there was a break, or intermission, in the service. The congregation retired to the "noonday house," a long, low building on the church grounds. The noonday house had a fireplace, and everyone crowded close to enjoy its warmth. Refreshments were served—hot brown bread, dough-nuts, or gingerbread. But even here talk and laughter were frowned upon. The children were herded together to hear a short sermon or to study Bible verses. Then it was time to file back into the church.

After the day's closing prayer, everyone waited respectfully until the minister and his family left the church. At last the congregation was free to rise and head for home. The long day of rest was over.

THE DEVIL AND HIS DISCIPLES

On a winter night in 1692, a group of teenage girls in Salem, Massa-chusetts, told each other's fortunes. They dropped the white of an egg into a glass of water and looked for signs and pictures in its swirling pattern. Today most people would see such a game as innocent fun. But these Puritan girls feared they were toying with real evil. Fortune-telling was the Devil's work. In the weeks that followed some of the girls were tormented by guilt and worry. They began to see strange visions and to feel pinches and pricks from unseen hands. Sometimes they fell to the floor, writhing and shrieking. Word flew through the town that the girls were bewitched.

Along with their deep faith in God, the English colonists brought another set of beliefs to the New World. Their notions about the dark powers of witchcraft dated back to the pre-Christian era in Europe. These pre-Christian, or pagan, beliefs blended with Christian ideas about Satan. The Puritans believed that Satan worked mischief on earth through disciples, or helpers. These helpers were witches who were granted evil powers. A witch could make a hen stop laying eggs, cause milk to turn sour, or make a child get sick. Anyone could become a witch by signing the Devil's great Black Book.

During the 1600s, hundreds of men and women were tried for witch-craft in New England. Witchcraft was one of the most serious crimes possible. The penalty was death.

People accused of witchcraft suffered terribly as a kind of fear and madness swept colonial New England.

A gravestone tells the sad end of one victim of the witchcraft trials.

How could a court of law decide whether someone was a witch or not? First the accused person (who was most often a woman) was examined for warts, moles, or other blemishes. Such marks could be signs that the person had been touched by the Devil. The accused person's neighbors were questioned closely. Had the accused ever uttered a curse or shaken a threatening finger? Afterward, had any accident occurred? Had anyone fallen ill?

Some witches were convicted on the basis of "spectral evidence." In these cases the witch's supposed victim testified that the "shape" of the accused appeared to him or her in a dream. In other words, if you saw your neighbor in a dream, and then something unpleasant happened to you in the morning, you could take your case before a judge. You could claim that your neighbor had put a curse on you.

THE WASHERWOMAN'S CURSE

One day in 1688 two Boston children, John and Martha Goodwin, collected the family's laundry from a washerwoman called the Widow Glover. The children complained to the widow that some of the clothes were missing. The widow cursed them for accusing her of stealing. Soon afterward the Goodwin children began to have strange convulsions. They told the court that the Widow Glover had put a curse on them. The washerwoman was hanged as a witch.

Between 1630 and 1692, sixteen convicted witches were hanged in Massachusetts and Connecticut. But the girls of Salem triggered a witchcraft hysteria that New England had never seen before. Ministers and judges asked them who was pinching and frightening them. The girls started to name their tormentors: a homeless woman, an African-American slave woman, even the town's former minister. More and more girls became afflicted, and more and more accusations were made. Soon the jails were full. The trials dragged on throughout the summer of 1692. Before the panic subsided, nineteen women and men were hanged in Salem. Another man was pressed to death with heavy stones for refusing to testify.

Witches were not the only wrongdoers to meet with severe punishment in early New England. The colonists employed stern measures to keep their communities running smoothly. Even so, people had a way of breaking the rules.

5
Community Spirit

"Robert Cole, having been oft punished for drunkenness, was now ordered to wear a red D about his neck for a year."

—JOURNAL OF JOHN WINTHROP, GOVERNOR OF THE MASSACHUSETTS BAY COLONY, 1634

CRIME AND PUNISHMENT

The early Puritan leaders had little tolerance for misbehavior. Drunkenness, lying, and gossip were among the numerous punishable crimes in New England. A visitor to Massachusetts in 1646 marveled that, "for kissing a woman in the street, though in way of civil salute, [one is punished with] whipping or a fine.…Scolds they gag and set them at their doors for certain hours, for all comers and goers by to gaze at."

Teachers used shame as a punishment for unruly schoolchildren. Public disgrace was also widely used as a punishment for adults. In addition to being whipped, a convicted person was often required to spend several hours in the stocks. The stocks was a wooden frame with openings for the person's arms and legs. The person was forced to sit or stand motionless in this device while passersby jeered and threw rotten vegetables. A similar contraption was called the pillory. The pillory clamped over the prisoner's neck and immobilized his or her head.

In many towns the stocks stood on the grassy public square, or common, in front of the meetinghouse. When needed, the gallows could be erected close by. Hangings were a public spectacle, attended by young and old. One day in 1653 such a large crowd attended a Boston execution that a drawbridge collapsed under the people's weight.

The conditions in colonial jails were appalling. Prisoners were often chained in filthy, airless cells. Unless their families provided them with food, they lived on dank water and wormy bread. As if this weren't punishment enough, prisoners were obliged to pay the jailers for room and board.

Today we are amazed that the colonists handed out such harsh punishments for trivial crimes. We ask ourselves how they could be so cruel in spite of their religious beliefs. Yet prisoners in the colonies fared better than those back in England, the mother country. In England a minor offender might have an ear cut off as a punishment. A man could be banished from his country forever simply for stealing food to feed his starving family. For more serious crimes one could be hanged, beheaded, or burned at the stake. New England justice was almost mild by comparison.

Ministers were among the most powerful people in Puritan society. In some cases, what they said from the pulpit soon became law.

GETTING THINGS DONE

William Bradford wanted to build a society united by faith. He trusted that each member would work willingly, not for personal gain but for the good of the community. Such cooperation soon proved an impossible dream. "The young men that were most able and fit for labor and service did repine that they should spend their time and strength to work for other men's wives and children without any recompense," Bradford wrote. "And for men's wives to be commanded to do service for other men, as dressing their meat, washing their clothes, they deemed it a

QUENCHING THE FLAMES

Each family in a New England town kept a large leather bucket in the common room. The bucket was tooled with initials, mottoes, or pictures. When the church bell tolled a fire alarm, the head of each household grabbed the bucket and rushed into the street. The townspeople formed a bucket brigade, passing pails of water from hand to hand to douse the flames. When the blaze was out, each family collected its own bucket, identified by its unique decorations.

A fire meant everyone lent a hand, or the
entire town would soon be in flames.

kind of slavery; neither could many husbands well brook it." Eventually each family was assigned its own plot of land for raising corn and other crops. People began to work harder. Everyone was happy with the new arrangement.

Though they farmed their own land and ran their own businesses, the New England colonists were dependent upon one another. Their sense of community was strengthened at monthly town meetings. These meetings were open to everyone, though only adult white men could vote. The town meetings gave the colonists a chance to raise concerns, offer new ideas, and air grievances. Officials chosen at town meetings played a major role in community life. Among them were the highway overseer, the fence viewer, and the public herdsman.

Highway overseers organized work crews to keep the roads in repair. Despite their efforts, New England roads were notoriously bad. A group of men in Lebanon, Connecticut, petitioned for improvements on the road they took to the meetinghouse on Sundays. They said they had to go through "particular men's [properties] as trespassers and through thirteen or fourteen fences and many miry places as well as over bad hills and be troublesome to our neighbors."

Away from the towns, the roads were even worse. They were little more than winding, rocky trails overhung with tangled branches. The few existing bridges were shaky and treacherous. Usually travelers crossed rivers on horseback or by a small boat that served as a ferry. A woman named Sarah Kemble Knight kept a journal of her trip from Boston to New York in 1704. She wrote of crossing a river in Rhode Island by canoe:

"The canoe was very small and shallow, so that when we were in she seemed ready to take in water, which greatly terrified me, and caused me to be very circumspect, sitting with my hands fast on each side, my eyes steady, not daring so much as to lodge my tongue a hair's breadth more on one side of my mouth than tother, nor so much as think on Lott's wife, for a wry thought would have overset [us]."

The fence viewer inspected fences to make certain that no one's pigs or goats could escape. When animals broke loose they could ravage a neighbor's crops. Some towns appointed a "hogreve." It was his job to capture and impound wandering pigs, much as a dogcatcher today rounds up stray dogs.

Since nearly everyone kept a cow or two, the public herdsman played an important role. At dawn he went through the town, collecting each cow and herding it to the common. There the cows of rich and poor munched the trampled grass side by side. At sundown, the herdsman drove the cows back through the streets, delivering each animal to the proper barn again.

The colonies did not maintain an army, but each town had its own military guard, or militia. The common was the militia's mustering ground. To the music of fife and drum the militia practiced maneuvers. If war broke out between the colonists and the Native Americans, this band of local men and boys was the town's only defense.

IN TIME OF SICKNESS

In the colonies, as in much of the world at that time, medicine was a blend of science, superstition, and folk wisdom. The colonists did their best to help one another when illness struck. Neighbors brought meals or sat with the sick person through the night. Someone was sure to drop in with a favorite remedy that had worked wonders in the past. One visitor to New England described a typical remedy for toothache:

"They boil gruel of flour of maize and milk. To this they add, whilst it is yet over the fire, some of the fat of hogs or other suet and stir it well, that everything mix equally. A handkerchief is then spread over the gruel and applied as hot as possible to the swelled cheek, where it is kept till it is gone cool again."

The colonists brought many European diseases with them to North America. Measles, smallpox, influenza, and diphtheria were especially devastating to the Indians. They had never encountered these diseases before and so had not had a chance to build up any natural immunities to them. Whole villages of Native Americans were wiped out by terrible epidemics. Sadly, most of the colonists felt this was to their advantage.

One Massachusetts official praised God for "sweeping away great multitudes of the natives by the smallpox a little before we went thither, that He might make room for us there."

Smallpox was a dreadful scourge for the colonists as well. A doctor described its effect on one of his patients: "The smallpox came out by the thousands on his face, which soon became one entire blister, and in two or three days after the body and limbs were beset with such numbers of them that the load bore down his strength before it in spite of every measure taken for his assistance."

Major smallpox epidemics struck New England every ten to fifteen

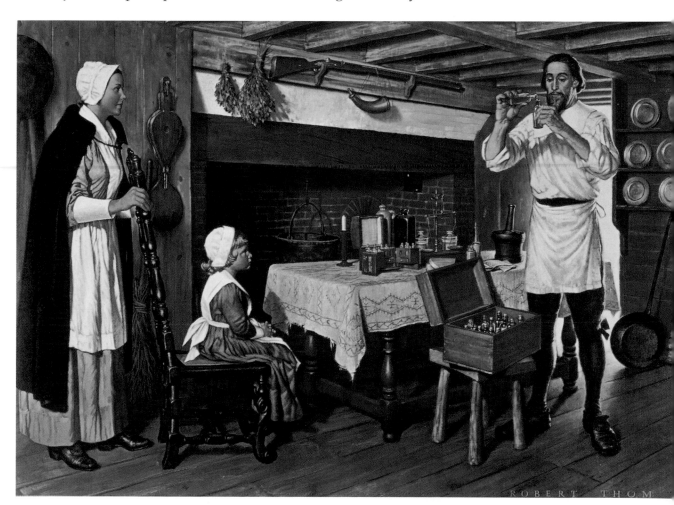

Home remedies were commonly used in colonial days.

LOST AND REVIVED

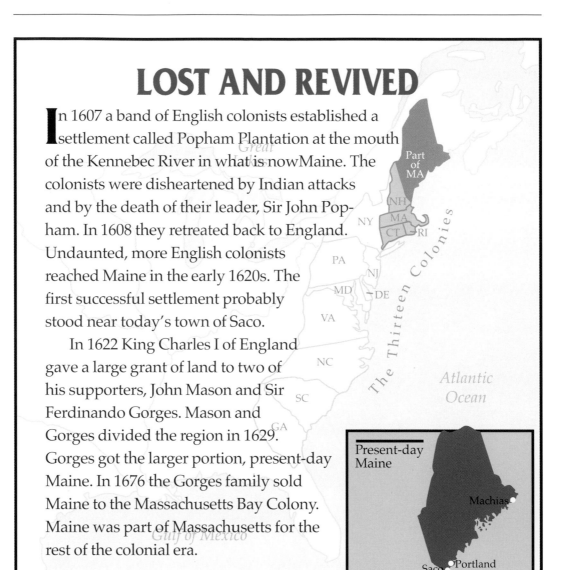

In 1607 a band of English colonists established a settlement called Popham Plantation at the mouth of the Kennebec River in what is now Maine. The colonists were disheartened by Indian attacks and by the death of their leader, Sir John Popham. In 1608 they retreated back to England. Undaunted, more English colonists reached Maine in the early 1620s. The first successful settlement probably stood near today's town of Saco.

In 1622 King Charles I of England gave a large grant of land to two of his supporters, John Mason and Sir Ferdinando Gorges. Mason and Gorges divided the region in 1629. Gorges got the larger portion, present-day Maine. In 1676 the Gorges family sold Maine to the Massachusetts Bay Colony. Maine was part of Massachusetts for the rest of the colonial era.

Part of MA

NH

NY   MA
CT   RI

PA

NJ

MD   DE

VA

NC

SC

GA

The Thirteen Colonies

Atlantic Ocean

Gulf of Mexico

Present-day Maine

Machias

Saco   Portland

years. In 1721 a Boston doctor named Zabdiel Boylston introduced the practice of inoculating healthy people against the disease. Inoculation had been used in Asia and Africa for centuries. African slaves suggested the idea to the colonists. Fluid was taken from the blister of a person with smallpox. With a needle a drop of this fluid was scratched into a healthy person's skin. The inoculated person usually got a mild form of the disease and was then protected from future attacks. The Reverend Cotton Mather staunchly supported inoculation, though most people feared that the practice would simply spread the disease. When Mather had his son inoculated he was assaulted by an angry mob.

Hardest hit by disease were the children. Nearly half of all the children born in colonial New England died before the age of ten. A woman from Ipswich, Massachusetts, wrote in her diary: "Here is an account of all my posterity: 6 sons and 3 daughters, 20 grandsons and 20 granddaughters, 58 in all. 33 are gone before me. I hope I shall meet them all at Christ's right hand among His sheep and lambs."

Their deep faith in God helped the New Englanders endure their crushing losses. Often they found comfort and pleasure in earthly things as well. They painted, wrote, and made music. Sometimes they even danced.

6
The Brightest Moments

"Our question is concerning…what is commonly called mixed or promiscuous dancing of men and women, be they elders or younger people, together. Now this we affirm to be utterly unlawful and that it cannot be tolerated in a place such as New England without great sin."

—INCREASE MATHER, BOSTON, 1684

MAKING MERRY

Reverend Increase Mather, father of the famous preacher Cotton Mather, lamented the growing popularity of dancing between men and women. But despite Mather's sermons, dancing had come to stay. At weddings and parties women and men frolicked to the lively strains of a fiddle. Sometimes they danced as partners. Sometimes they formed a circle or a twisting line. But always they had fun, regardless of the preachers' warnings.

From the earliest days of Plymouth Plantation some New Englanders flouted the strict teachings of their leaders. During the 1620s one band of colonists established a settlement called Merry Mount. There they danced, drank rum, sang "bawdy ballads," and consorted with the Indians. The Pilgrims were shocked when the people of Merry Mount set up a maypole and danced around it with their Indian friends.

The Puritans felt that religious holidays should be treated with respect, and frowned on frivolous celebrations. It was better to ignore the holiday altogether than to mark it with dancing and parties. Judge Samuel Sewall was aghast when Bostonians turned to revelry on Shrove Tuesday, the day before the start of Lent for Roman Catholics and members of the Church of England. In his diary Sewall noted that one townsman "carries a cock at his back with a bell in his hand in the main street. Several follow him blindfold and under pretense of striking him or his cock with great cart-whips strike passengers and make great disturbance."

To the most devout Puritans, nothing could be more frivolous than the theater. There men and women pretended to be what they were not. Stage plays filled the audience with dangerous fancies. Yet as the years slipped by, even the theater gained a toehold in the stony soil of New England. In 1761 a traveling troupe of players arrived in Newport, Rhode Island, with a production of Shakespeare's Othello. To make the show acceptable to New Englanders it was advertised as A SERIES OF MORAL DIALOGUES, IN FIVE PARTS, DEPICTING THE EVIL EFFECTS OF JEALOUSY AND OTHER BAD PASSIONS, AND PROVING THAT

HAPPINESS CAN ONLY SPRING FROM THE PURSUIT OF VIRTUE.

Only the strictest New Englanders shunned music. The violin, or fiddle, was connected with dancing, and was not always encouraged in polite society. However, many other instruments were considered proper entertainment on social occasions. Girls sometimes studied the virginal, an instrument resembling the piano. Young men learned to play the trumpet or the clarinet. Singers could be accompanied on the lute, a stringed instrument in the guitar family.

THE JOY OF WORDS

Books were rare treasures to the New England colonists. Most families owned a cherished copy of the Bible, and perhaps a collection of sermons by one of the famous Puritan ministers. In addition, the colonists prized books on law, medicine, and history. Most of these books were written and published in England.

This is the first known drawing of Harvard University, in 1726. Before the school was founded in 1636, students went to college in England.

In 1638 one New Englander, John Harvard, donated his precious collection of books to a newly opened college in Cambridge, Massachusetts. In gratitude the college trustees named the school in his honor. Today Harvard University is one of the world's most renowned institutions of higher learning.

The first book published in New England, or for that matter anywhere in the thirteen English colonies, was *The Bay Psalm-Book*, which appeared in 1640. It was a translation of several of the biblical Psalms, arranged to be sung in church services. In 1702 Cotton Mather published Magnali Christi Americana, a history of Puritan New England. In the introduction he explains, "I write the wonders of the Christian religion, flying from the depravations of Europe, to the American strand: and, assisted by the Holy Author of that religion, I do…report the wonderful displays of His infinite power…wherewith His Divine Providence has irradiated an Indian wilderness." Mather published more than four hundred works on religion, philosophy, and science. He was the most learned person in the New England colonies, and amassed a library of more than three thousand books.

Few women had a chance to become educated during the colonial era. Yet the two best-known poets of the New England colonies were women, Anne Bradstreet and Phillis Wheatley. Anne Bradstreet (1612-1672) was born in England and came to Massachusetts with her husband when she was eighteen. Though she had eight children she managed to find time to write. Most of her poems have religious themes. In her poem "The Prologue,"she addresses the problems she faces as a female poet:

"I am obnoxious to each carping tongue
Who says my hand a needle better fits,
A poet's pen all scorn I should thus wrong
For such despite they cast on female wits."

Phillis Wheatley (1753?-1784) was born in Africa and was brought to Boston as a slave when she was eight years old. Slavery was not widespread in New England, but some families kept slaves as house servants. Phillis was purchased by a merchant named John Wheatley. The Wheatleys took an interest in her and taught her to read and write. When she was fourteen she began writing poems. A collection of her work, *Poems on Various Subjects, Religious and Moral*, was published in England in 1773. Years later a strong antislavery movement sprang up in New England. Phillis Wheatley's poems helped to show the world what African Americans could achieve when given the opportunity.

THINGS OF BEAUTY

Out of necessity the colonists were practical people. During the 1600s they had little time for painting pictures or making statues. Yet their tools, utensils, and furniture were made with such loving care that they were artistic creations. The arm of a chair might be carved with flowers and leaves. Initials might curl around the rim of a wooden trencher. Pewter dishes and mugs combined graceful form with a fine luster.

In her poem "To the Right Honorable William, Earl of Dartmouth," Phillis Wheatley argued that just like the American colonies, slaves wished to be free.

Among the craftspeople of colonial New England, none commanded greater respect than the silversmiths. Customers provided the silver, usually in the form of old Spanish coins. The coins were melted down and

THE MIDNIGHT RIDER

Paul Revere of Boston (1735-1818) is best remembered as the man who warned that the British were coming at the start of the American War for Independence. But long before his midnight ride, Revere was famous as the best silversmith in New England. In addition to making tableware, he created false teeth. One of his advertisements promised that they would look "as well as the natural and answer the end [purpose] of speaking."

Paul Revere, master silversmith, in a painting by John Singleton Copley

shaped into exquisite spoons, platters, and pitchers. Silver-smiths took pride in their work, and usually marked it with their initials. Today collectors pay huge sums for the work of Boston masters such as John Hull and Robert Sanderson.

Making quilts gave women and girls the chance to express their creativity. By stitching together colorful scraps of fabric or "stuff," New England women formed intricate and original patterns. The making of a large quilt required many hands. Several women gathered in someone's home and worked together through a happy after-noon. Such quilts became treasured heirlooms, passed from mother to daughter for generations.

The portrait of a parent or a child was another valued family possession. Traveling artists

A traveling artist, known as a limner, made this painting of a colonial New England woman. The artist probably only added her face to the already completed body.

went from door to door with bundles of canvases. On each was a partially completed picture, lacking only the face. When a farmer or merchant ordered a portrait, the painter simply filled in the face of the person in question. Few of these portraits would win prizes in an art competition. But they brightened the lives of women and men in the backcountry of Vermont, Maine, and western Massachusetts.

By the 1700s, more sophisticated artists appeared in Boston, Newport, and other cities. Robert Feke (1705?-1750?) painted the portraits of several wealthy Boston and Newport citizens. John Singleton Copley (1738-1815) established his reputation in Boston before he moved to Europe in 1774. Today most critics agree that he did his best work while he lived in Massachusetts. His *Boy with a Squirrel* is the lively portrait of a New England boy with a pet squirrel on a chain.

By the late 1700s, the New England colonists had established an identity of their own. They had their own art and literature. Their recipes and remedies were unique. Many colonists no longer thought of themselves as British subjects. They were becoming Americans.

In 1776 the New England colonies joined with the colonies to the south to declare political independence from Great Britain. Seven years later, after a long and bitter war, the thirteen former colonies merged to form one sovereign nation.

The colonial era was over at last. But in New England its memories linger along back roads and city streets. The headstones in an old churchyard and the steep roof of a country cottage offer tempting glimpses of the way people lived in the colonies long ago.

THE GREEN MOUNTAIN

Though Vermont is considered part of New England today, it was not one of the original thirteen colonies. The French explorer Samuel de Champlain claimed the region for France in 1609. He gave it the name Vermont, meaning "Green Mountain." In 1724 a band of settlers from Massachusetts built a fort near present-day Brattleboro as a defense against Indian raiding parties. But Vermont remained in French hands until 1763. As a condition of the treaty that ended the French and Indian War (1754-1763), a vast tract of land, including Vermont, was granted to Great Britain.

Glossary

affirm: To insist upon.

antimony: A bluish white mineral used to make pewter.

bawdy ballad: Coarse or indecent song.

carping: Complaining.

chartered: Given a written document, called a charter, that explains certain rights and obligations. A charter is given by a government or ruler to a person, group of people, or a company. In colonial New England, the king of England issued charters to people who wanted to establish towns and colonies.

consort: To associate in a free and easy fashion.

deacon: A church official.

depravation: Evil, immorality.

dissenter: One who opposes a widely accepted belief or practice.

flout: To openly defy.

frivolous: Lighthearted; lacking in substance or purpose.

gruel: A thin porridge made of flour or cornmeal.

heathen: A person who does not believe in the God of the Christians, Jews, or Muslims.

heirloom: A treasured object handed down in a family.

inoculation: The practice of giving a healthy person or animal a small amount of a substance that contains weakened disease germs in order to help the body protect itself against the disease.

irradiate: To fill with light.

loathsome: Hideous, disgusting.

lug pole: A heavy bar at the back of a fireplace, from which pots and kettles can hang over the flames.

miry: Marshy.

obnoxious: Offensive.

pewter: A metal made by blending a small amount of copper and antimony with tin.

quench: To make something stop burning; put out; extinguish.

recompense: Reward or payment.

repine: To lament.

revelry: Wild merrymaking.

scourge: Something that causes widespread pain or punishment.

skewer: To pierce through.

spindle: Part of a spinning wheel, a slender wooden cylinder for twisting fibers into thread.

spit: Metal prong on which meat is turned above a fire.

staple: A very important product or crop in a region, one that most people need or use.

suet: A strip of fat removed from meat.

tow: Rough, inexpensive fabric once made from coarse linen thread.

translucent: Allowing some light to pass through.

treacherous: Dangerous, untrustworthy.

trencher: A carved wooden dish or bowl.

A NOTE ABOUT SPELLING

If you were to read a letter or diary written in colonial days, you would be amazed by the way some of the words are spelled. The word wind might be spelled wynd or wynde. Words would be capitalized almost at random. Until the middle of the 1700s, English-language spelling had few standard rules. People spelled words more or less as they wished. The results are certainly interesting, but they can be confusing, too. To clarify the meaning for the readers of this book, I have modernized the spelling in all quotes from colonial documents.

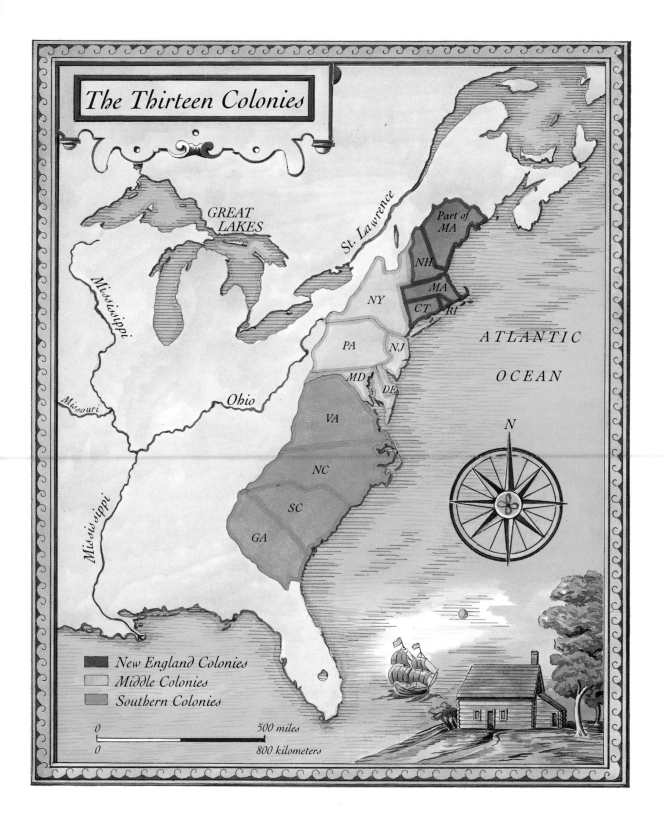

The Thirteen Colonies

GREAT LAKES

St. Lawrence

Mississippi

Missouri

Ohio

Mississippi

Part of MA

NH

NY

MA

CT

RI

PA

NJ

MD

DE

VA

NC

SC

GA

ATLANTIC

OCEAN

N

New England Colonies
Middle Colonies
Southern Colonies

0   500 miles
0   800 kilometers

Colonial New England in Time

1607—English colonists settle at Popham Plantation near the mouth of the Kennebec River in present-day Maine; they return to England the following year.

1609—The French explorer Samuel de Champlain claims most of present-day Vermont for France.

1620—A small band of English colonists called the Separatists founds Plymouth Plantation in present-day Massachusetts; they are remembered today as the Pilgrims who celebrated the first Thanksgiving.

1623—David Thomson establishes the first English settlement in New Hampshire, near the present-day town of Rye; English colonists return to Maine and establish permanent settlements.

1630—The Massachusetts Bay Colony is founded at Boston by a group of English Puritans.

1633—Colonists from Massachusetts found the town of Windsor, Connecticut.

1636—Roger Williams is driven out of Massachusetts and founds Providence in present-day Rhode Island; Harvard College is founded in Cambridge, Massachusetts, to train young men for the clergy.

1640—*The Bay Psalm-Book* appears, the first book published in the English colonies.

1675—Hostilities between the colonists and the Indians erupt in King Philip's War.

1721—Dr. Zabdiel Boylston of Boston introduces the practice of inoculation against smallpox.

1724—Colonists from Massachusetts establish a settlement near present-day Brattleboro, Vermont.

1741—Jonathan Edwards preaches his terrifying sermon "Sinners in the Hands of an Angry God" during an intense revival of Puritanism known as the Great Awakening.

1754–1763—France and Great Britain, each with Indian allies, battle over territory in North America. The conflict is known as the French and Indian War. Great Britain is victorious and gains a vast tract of land, including Vermont.

1776—Delegates from the thirteen British colonies sign the Declaration of Independence, calling for a break with the mother country.

1783—The former colonies become an independent nation, the United States.

Places to Visit

CONNECTICUT

Putnam Cottage, Greenwich:
This house was built in 1690. On the grounds is an herb garden that displays many of the medicinal plants once used by the colonists.

Whitfield House, Guilford:
Built in 1639, this is the oldest house in New England. It has been restored to look much as it did in the seventeenth century.

MAINE

Burnham Tavern, Machias:
In 1775 colonists gathered here to plot the capture of the British ship Margaretta. The same sign has greeted guests since 1770: "Drink for the thirsty, food for the hungry, lodging for the weary, and good keeping for the horses."

Tate House, Portland:
This restored eighteenth-century house is the oldest building in Portland. Among its features is the outbuilding that once served as slave quarters.

MASSACHUSETTS

Faneuil Hall Marketplace, Boston:
This two-story building with its striking bronze dome was Boston's central market after 1742. Before the War of Independence, patriots often gathered in meeting rooms on the second floor. Today Faneuil Hall is an indoor mall with dozens of stores and restaurants.

Hancock-Clarke House, Lexington:
After he left the Old North Church, Paul Revere rode to this house to warn colonial leaders John Hancock and Samuel Adams that the British were on their way. The house has stood here since 1698. It contains period furnishings, portraits, and other colonial memorabilia.

Old North Church, Boston:
On the night of April 18, 1775, Paul Revere climbed to the tower of this church and hung two lanterns as a signal that the British were coming. This incident is immortalized in Henry Wadsworth Longfellow's poem "Paul Revere's Ride." The Old North Church was completed in 1723 and is the oldest church in Boston.

Paul Revere House, Boston:
Built in 1680, this is the last surviving seventeenth-century house in downtown Boston. Revere lived here when he made his famous ride in 1775. The house contains art and furnishings from the seventeenth and eighteenth centuries. Several examples of Revere's silverwork are also on display.

*Pilgrim Monument and Museum,
Provincetown:*
A 250-foot granite tower commemorates
the landing of the Separatists, or Pilgrims,
near this site in 1620. The museum contains
maps, pictures, and other memorabilia of
the Plymouth Colony.

Pioneer Village, Salem:
Pioneer Village is the re-creation of the
Puritan settlement that stood here in 1630.
Visitors can explore "English wigwams"
and thatched houses. Guides in period
costumes demonstrate crafts from early
New England.

Plymouth Plantation, Plymouth:
A reconstruction of the first English
settlement in Massachusetts as it appeared
in 1627. Staff members wear period
costumes and speak as the colonists did,
in Elizabethan English. The Mayflower II,
a replica of the Pilgrims' original vessel,
floats at anchor off the shore.

Rebecca Nurse Homestead, Danvers:
This house, built in 1680, is typical of the
"saltbox" style of colonial New England
architecture. It was the home of Rebecca
Nurse, one of the women executed during
the witchcraft trials of 1692. Among the
homestead's outbuildings is the replica
of a 1672 meetinghouse.

Salem Witch Museum, Salem:
This museum brings the Salem witch
trials to life through a dramatic multi-
media presentation. Special programs are
planned around the Halloween season.

Witch House, Salem:
In 1692 this was the home of Jonathan
Corwin, one of the judges in the infamous
Salem witch trials. Several of the accused
witches were brought here for questioning.
The house has been restored to look as it
did in 1692.

NEW HAMPSHIRE
Strawbery Banke, Portsmouth:
This ten-acre waterfront complex includes
forty-two restored historic buildings. The
oldest dates back to 1695. Visitors can
watch demonstrations of spinning,
weaving, and other colonial crafts.

RHODE ISLAND
*Gilbert Stuart Birthplace,
North Kingstown:*
This house, built in 1751, was the
birthplace of one of America's most noted
early painters. It has been fully restored
with furnishings from the late eighteenth
century. Nearby stands a gristmill where
the colonists once took corn to be ground
into meal.

VERMONT
Old Constitution House, Windsor:
This house was built in 1772 as a tavern
for travelers. Vermont's first constitution
was written here in 1777.

To Learn More...

BOOKS

Hakim, Joy. *Making Thirteen Colonies.* New York: Oxford University Press, 1993.

Kent, Deborah. *African-Americans in the Thirteen Colonies.* Danbury, CT: Children's Press, 1996.

Penner, Lucille Recht. *Eating the Plates: A Pilgrim Book of Food and Manners.* New York: Macmillan, 1991.

Sherrow, Victoria. *Huskings, Quiltings, and Barn Raisings: Work-Play Parties in Early America.* New York: Walker, 1992.

Smith, Carter, ed. *Daily Life: A Sourcebook on Colonial America.* Brookfield, CT: Millbrook, 1992.

Tunis, Edwin. *Colonial Living.* New York: Crowell, 1957.

Warner, John F. *Colonial American Home Life.* New York: Franklin Watts, 1993.

Washburne, Carolyn Kott. A *Multicultural Portrait of Colonial Life.* Tarrytown, NY: Marshall Cavendish, 1994.

AUDIO AND VIDEO

Colonial and Revolution Songs, with Historical Narration, by Keith and Rusty McNeil. Two 60-minute audiocassettes. Contain a variety of songs from throughout the thirteen colonies. Wem Records, Riverside, CA, 1993.

Early Settlers. One 25-minute videocassette. Told from a child's point of view, describes life in colonial Massachusetts and Virginia. Schlessinger Video Productions, Bala Cynwyd, PA, 1995.

Slavery and Freedom. One 35-minute videocassette. Covers indentured servitude and slavery in the New World. Schlessinger Video Productions, Bala Cynwyd, PA, 1996.

WEBSITES*

Massachusetts History, http://ftp.std.com/NE/mahistory.html Information about the Puritans, the full text of the Mayflower Compact, and a guide to Plymouth Plantation.

Websites change from time to time. For additional on-line information, check with your media specialist at your local library.

Bibliography

Bridenbaugh, Carl. *Cities in the Wilderness: The First Century of Urban Life in America, 1625-1742*. New York: Knopf, 1954.

Demos, John. *The Unredeemed Captive: A Family Story from Early America*. New York: Knopf, 1994.

Earle, Alice Morse. *Child Life in Colonial Days*. Stockbridge, MA: Berkshire House, 1993. (Originally published by Macmillan, New York, 1899.)

———. *Home Life in Colonial Days*. Stockbridge, MA: Berkshire House, 1993. (Originally published by Macmillan, New York, 1898.)

Encyclopedia Britannica, ed. *The Annals of America*. Vol. 1, *1493-1754, Discovering a New World*. Chicago: Encyclopedia Britannica, 1976.

Hawke, David Freeman. *Everyday Life in Early America*. New York: Harper & Row, 1988.

Langdon, William Chauncy. *Everyday Things in Early America, 1607-1776*. New York: Scribners, 1938.

Lockridge, Kenneth A. *A New England Town: The First Hundred Years, Dedham, Massachusetts, 1636-1736*. New York: W. W. Norton, 1985.

Rae, Noel, ed. *Witnessing America: The Library of Congress Book of Firsthand Accounts of Life in America, 1600-1900*. New York: Penguin, 1996.

Reisch, Jerome R. *Colonial America*. Englewood Cliffs, NJ: Prentice-Hall, 1994.

Ulrich, Laurel Thatcher. *Good Wives: Image and Reality in the Lives of Women in Northern New England, 1650-1750*. New York: Knopf, 1982.

Wright, Lewis B. *The Cultural Life of the American Colonies, 1607-1763*. New York: Harper & Row, 1957.

Notes on Quotes

The quotations from this book are from the following sources:

A Stern and Rock-Bound Coast
Page 7, "In two or three months' time": Encyclopedia Britannica, *The Annals of America*, Vol. 1, p. 66.

Home and Hearth
Page 13, "The chimney is large": Earle, *Home Life in Colonial Days*, p. 54.

Page 19, "Sowed peas; sweet marjoram": Ulrich, *Good Wives*, p. 70.

Seen and Not Heard
Page 25, "Surely there is in all children": Earle, *Child Life in Colonial Days*, p. 192.

Page 26, "She hath never been whipped before": *Child Life in Colonial Days*, p. 207.

Page 26, "Richard wears out nigh 12 pair of shoes": *Child Life in Colonial Days*, p. 88.

Page 29, "Try to mend your hand": *Child Life in Colonial Days*, p. 159.

Page 30, "[The boy] must rise early": *Child Life in Colonial Days*, p. 307–308.

Commanded by the Lord
Page 33, "The God that holds you over the pit of Hell": *The Annals of America*, p. 429.

Page 34, "Though I am thus well in body": *Child Life in Colonial Days*, pp. 239–240.

Page 36, "smiling and laughing and enticing": *Home Life in Colonial Days*, p. 373.

Community Spirit
Page 43, "Robert Cole, having been oft punished for drunkenness": Rae, *Witnessing America*, p. 409.

Page 44, "For kissing a woman in the street": *Witnessing America*, p. 413.

Page 45, "The young men that were most able": *The Annals of America*, p. 73.

Page 47, "particular men's [properties] as trespassers": Langdon, *Everyday Things in Early America*, p. 242.

Page 47, "The canoe was very small and shallow": *Everyday Things in Early America*, p. 246.

Page 48, "They boil gruel of flour of maize": Hawke, *Everyday Life in Early America*, p. 84.

Page 49, "sweeping away great multitudes": *The Annals of America*, p. 178.

Page 49, "The smallpox came out by the thousands": *The Annals of America*, p. 81.

Page 51, "Here is an account of all my posterity": *Good Wives*, p. 149.

The Brightest Moments
Page 53, "Our question is concerning": *The Annals of America*, p. 278.

Page 54, "carries a cock at his back": Wright, *The Cultural Life of the American Colonies*, p. 189.

Page 54, "A SERIES OF MORAL DIALOGUES": *Witnessing America*, p. 321.

Page 56, "I write the wonders of the Christian religion": Bartlett, *Bartlett's Familiar Quotations*, p. 319.

Page 56, "I am obnoxious to each carping tongue": *The Annals of America*, p. 198.

Page 58, "as well as the natural": *The Cultural Life of the American Colonies*, p. 214

Index

About the Author

Deborah Kent grew up in Little Falls, New Jersey, and received her Bachelor of Arts degree from Oberlin College in Ohio. She went on to earn a Master's Degree from Smith College School for Social Work and took a job at the University Settlement House in New York City. After four years in social work, she decided to pursue her lifelong interest in writing. She moved to San Miguel de Allende, Mexico, a charming town with a colony of foreign writers and artists. In San Miguel she wrote her first novel for young adults, *Belonging*.

Today Deborah has more than a dozen novels to her credit, and has written many nonfiction children's books as well. She lives in Chicago with her husband, children's book author R. Conrad Stein, and their daughter, Janna.

"When I was in school," Deborah recalls, "I thought history was boring. We learned about wars and political leaders, but seldom heard about ordinary people. Back then I could never have guessed that some day I would study history for fun, and that I would even write books about it! I am fascinated not by generals and presidents, but by the women, men, and children of the past whose names have been nearly forgotten. It is exciting to explore the world they knew and to try to imagine how they lived their lives."